Creative Ribbon Embroidery

Frontispiece—'The Yellow Garden' by Kath Chate

Creative
Ribbon
Embroidery

Heather Joynes

Kangaroo Press

Conversion table from metric to inches for use in this book:

10 mm = 1 cm
1 cm = $\frac{3}{8}$ inch
5 cm = 2 inches
0.5 m = 50 cm = 19$\frac{3}{4}$ inches
1 metre = 39$\frac{3}{8}$ inches

Where the requirements state 1 metre, 1 yard should be sufficient. When buying ribbons, 2 metres is a useful quantity.

Front Cover—'Florist's Window'

Reprinted 1990
First published in 1989 by Kangaroo Press Pty Ltd
3 Whitehall Road (P.O. Box 75) Kenthurst 2156
Typeset by G.T. Setters Pty Limited
Printed in Singapore by Kyodo Printing

ISBN 0 86417 263 X

Contents

Introduction

Creative Ribbon Embroidery contains further developments in the technique introduced in *Ribbon Embroidery*, and ideas and designs for a variety of items.

Although I prefer to encourage people to design their own work, I realise there are many who are more comfortable with a design prepared for them. I have therefore included a number of design diagrams for various items in this book.

I hope that anyone using these designs will feel free to alter them, changing colours, materials or stitches. Everyone can add their own creative touch to a design. The designs can be adapted to suit many things other than the specific items illustrated.

The addition of stitchery in threads adds a lighter texture to the richness of ribbons and gives the work contrast and balance.

Unless otherwise stated the embroidery, photographs and diagrams are all the work of the author.

Materials

These days a vast choice of materials is available, and many are suitable bases for ribbon embroidery. Firm fabrics give the best results. Velveteen and dress velvet are rich and good to work on, but avoid heavy furnishing velvets as they are too thick and difficult to pull ribbon through. If you are working on fine silk, back it with a piece of silk organza to give the fabric more body. If you wish to use velvet ribbon pulled through fabric choose a more loosely woven fabric, in wool, cotton or linen. Otherwise, use the velvet ribbon on the surface of the fabric only.

The range of polyester, satin, nylon, silk and velvet ribbons makes ribbon embroidery very exciting. Combinations of different textures in ribbons can be most effective, using shiny satins with matt silk or nylon. There are also many fashion ribbons which come and go. If any of the ribbons that appear in this book are not available in your area, use your imagination with what is available. Sometimes this can generate an idea that leads to exciting new designs.

When buying ribbons without a specific purpose in mind two or three metres is a useful quantity. The most practical way to store ribbons is on small rolled cards. Business cards are a convenient size, with a cut in each short end to hold the ends of the ribbon. The card is rolled and held with adhesive tape. Keep each range of colour separate, either in large divided boxes or in a box for each colour. Winding ribbon around flat cards is not recommended as it makes creases in the ribbon.

The most useful threads are Perle cotton Nos 5 and 8 and stranded cotton, but there are many beautiful embroidery threads that can enhance embroidery with ribbons. Silk threads and very shiny rayon threads can add a particularly good contrast. You will need sewing cotton to match the ribbons used.

Various types of needles in several sizes are essential—tapestry needles, which have a large eye and blunt point, chenille needles, also large eyed, but with sharp points, and crewel needles, which have a long eye. The finer sizes of crewel needle, 9 to 12, are the most useful.

Good embroidery scissors and a larger pair will be needed, and a stiletto or awl for piercing holes in the fabric to pull the ribbon through. An antique stiletto in steel, bone or ivory is very nice to use if you can obtain one.

An embroidery hoop can be used, but take care that the hoop does not mark the fabric, particularly if working on velvet.

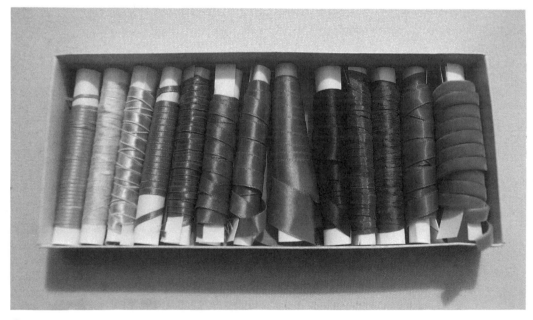

Ribbons rolled on card rolls

Starting and Finishing

To start, leave about 1.5 cm of ribbon on the wrong side of the work. This is sewn down with sewing cotton when part of the work is completed. Finish in the same way. It is essential not to leave long ends behind the work as they will tangle. Some polyester ribbons are very springy and need to be sewn down at the back of the work as soon as is practical.

If it is difficult to pull a ribbon through the fabric, use a stiletto to pierce a hole for the ribbon to pass through.

When pulling the ribbon through to the back of the work check to see that the needle is not piercing a ribbon already worked, as this can make it difficult to pull through, and will distort the work.

Designs

The design must be suitable in scale for the article you are making. Always establish the size and shape of the article first, then the area to be embroidered, then the details of the design. Details of the design need only be simple, e.g. circles and ovals for flowers and leaves.

Designing for clothing needs special attention as the whole garment has to be considered as well as the person who will wear it.

Cut an extra pattern in paper and mark on it the area to be embroidered, then try it against the person who will wear it. Any adjustments can be made before working up the design of the embroidery.

If it is an important garment it is worth making a calico replica with the design marked on it. Time spent on planning and designing is time well spent and will save hours of anguished unpicking.

When working on anything with seams that will be under the embroidery, work on each piece of the article to within about 3 cm of the seam, sew up the seams, press on the wrong side then complete the embroidery over the seam.

Transferring Designs

Only a very simple outline of the design needs to be transferred to the fabric to be embroidered.

For small pieces such as brooches or needle cases you need only mark the placement of the largest elements of the design with a dot in pencil or water soluble fabric marking pen. The rest of the design can be followed from the drawing.

For larger or more specific designs, outline the design on paper with a black felt pen so that it is very clear. Tape this to a flat surface with adhesive tape. Lay a piece of nylon net over the design and attach it with adhesive tape. Go over the outline of the design with a black marking pen, then remove the net and place in position on the fabric to be embroidered. Pin or baste securely in place. Now go over the outline on the net with a water soluble fabric marking pen. When you remove the net, the outline of the design will appear on your fabric as a series of dots. These dots can be removed when the embroidery is finished by holding a cotton bud damped with water against them.

When transferring a design from a book by this method, place a piece of firm clear plastic over the design before tracing it with a felt pen.

Finishing

Your finished ribbon embroidery can be pressed lightly, on the wrong side, into a well padded surface—a folded towel is ideal. Take care not to flatten the embroidery.

When mounting pictures, make sure the mount is perfectly squared at the corners. If possible, use acid free board.

When working with glue, work with clean scrap paper and change the paper at every stage of the construction.

A large darning needle is ideal for spreading glue and for applying a small spot of glue to a small area.

Stitches

Make stitches large enough for the scale of the ribbon and work rather more loosely than usual.

Make sure the needle is large enough to take the ribbon comfortably.

If you want the ribbon flat, hold it in place with your thumb while pulling it through the fabric. It can sometimes be effective to let the ribbon twist.

Use stitches that have most of the stitch on the right side of the work—herringbone, chain and cretan stitches all have a minimum of the stitch on the reverse side.

Stitches threaded with ribbons can make rich patterns. Use a firm thread such as Perle cotton for the groundwork stitch. A great many effects can be achieved with straight stitches, particularly when working flowers, as you will see from the illustrations in the book.

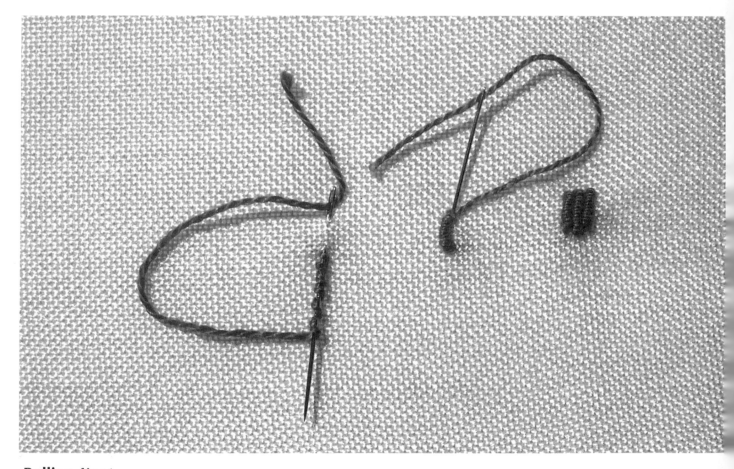

Bullion Knot

A most useful stitch for centres of flowers, wheat ears, small leaves, etc.

1. Make a stitch as shown, bringing the eye of the needle almost through the fabric.

2. Wind the thread around several times, depending how long the stitch is to be.

3. Pull the needle and thread through the twists, holding the twists firmly in one hand.

4. Take the needle down as shown, to complete the stitch.

Buttonhole Stitch

Bring the needle and thread out on the line of the lower edge of the stitch. Make a stitch as shown, with the thread looped under the needle.

At the right of the picture, two rows of buttonhole stitch are shown worked brick fashion.

This is a very versatile stitch and can be worked well spaced, as shown, closely or unevenly.

A circle of closely worked buttonhole stitch makes a round flower.

Detached Chain Stitch

This stitch can be worked with a short or long stitch at the end.

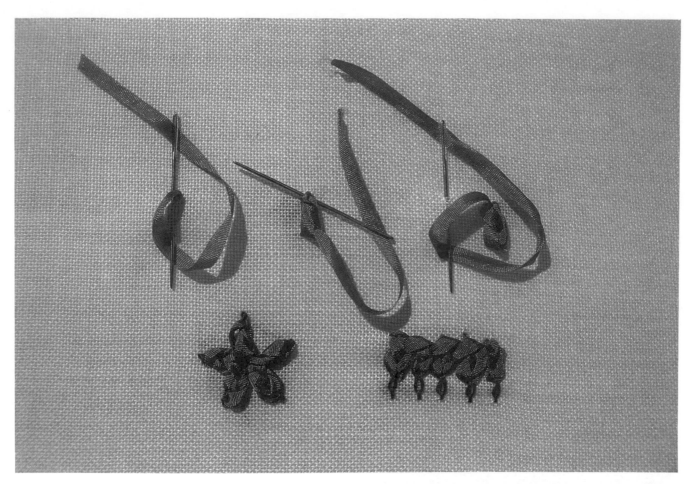

Rosette Chain Stitch

This stitch is worked from right to left.

1. Work a twisted chain stitch.

2. Pass the needle under the top of the stitch, taking care not to pull it up tightly.

This is rather a loose stitch and really needs another small stitch at the end to hold it down. There are two ideas illustrated—the row of stitches has a small chain stitch on the end, and the flower is finished with a French knot.

Twisted Chain Stitch

The needle goes into the fabric over the thread before making the chain. In ribbon this stitch makes a good bud.

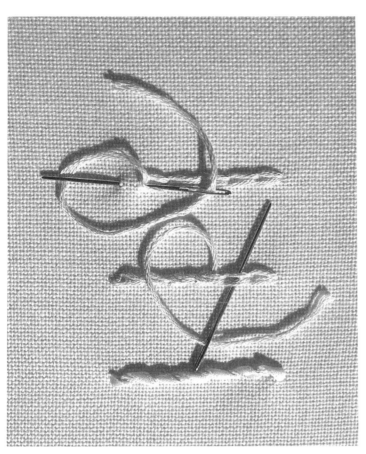

Whipped Chain Stitch

Work a row of continuous chain stitch then whip over each stitch with the same thread or a contrasting colour.

Couching

Lay a piece of ribbon along the line to be covered, and with another thread, tie it down with a small stitch at intervals.

Cretan Stitch (left)

Note that the needle always points inwards, with the thread under it. Cretan stitch is very versatile as it can be worked closely or spaced evenly or unevenly, so that many different textures can be created with it.

Fly Stitch (facing page)

This is a most versatile stitch and can be worked singly, in groups with long or short tails, in horizontal or vertical rows. It is very good for ferns or feathery foliage.

Cross Stitch (below)

This can be worked as a straight or diagonal cross. A cross in the opposite direction can be worked over the centre in a finer thread. In clusters, cross stitch makes an attractive group of small flowers.

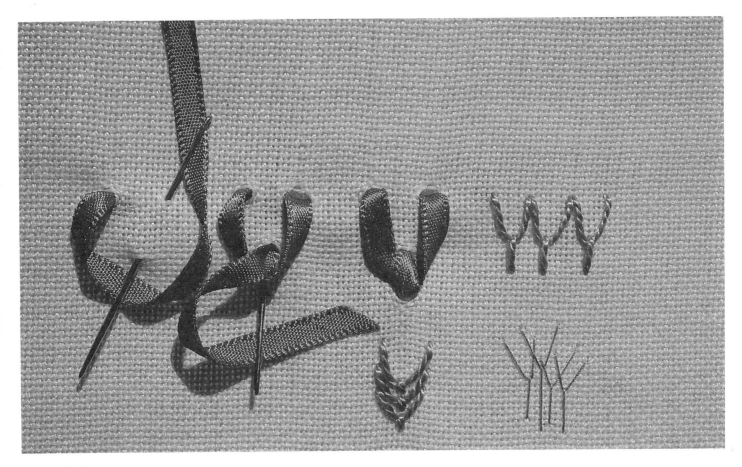

French Knot (below)

1. Bring the thread or ribbon through to the front of the work, twist it once only around the needle, pull snugly around the needle, then insert the needle into the fabric close to the starting point and pull through to the back.

2. Hold the thread firmly with the thumb while pulling through. When working with satin ribbon leave the knot slightly looser than normal while pulling the ribbon through to the back.

A long tailed French knot is shown at the right in the illustration. For this, after twisting the thread round the needle, take it down to the length required and finish the stitch in the usual way.

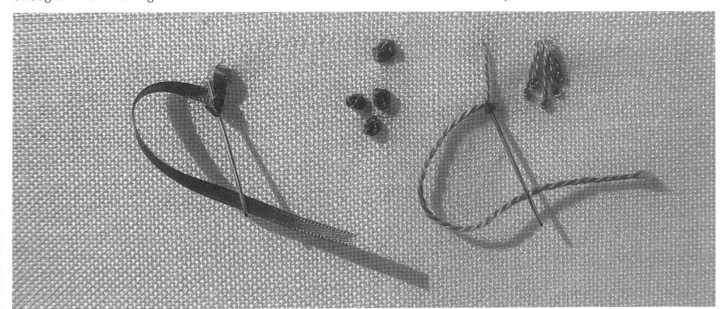

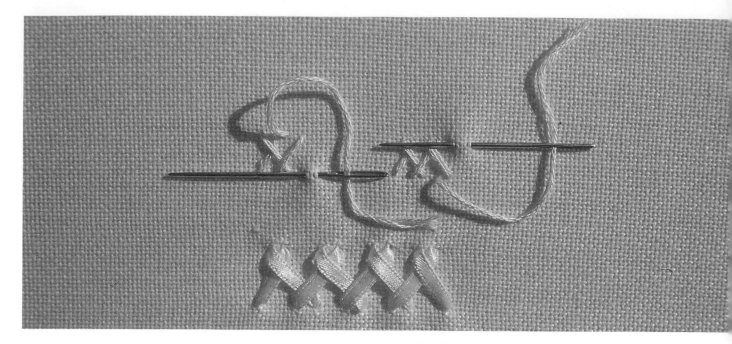

Herringbone Stitch *(above)*

This stitch can be worked very close or well spaced.

It is ideal for working over ribbon on a curved line. It also looks very effective worked in Perle cotton and threaded with ribbon.

Raised Stem Band *(below)*

1. First work a 'ladder' of straight stitches as shown at the left.

2. Then work stem stitch over these bars, not going through the fabric. Work rows side by side, placing them closely until the whole ladder is filled.

3. The rows may be worked all in the same direction or up and down.

For a rounded effect, work a padding of straight stitches in wool yarn under the bars before working the stem stitch.

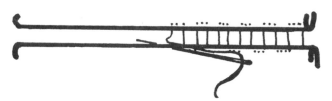

Ladder Stitch

This is a very good method to stitch two pieces together on the right side.

Pick up the fold on the seam line with the needle, bring the needle and thread through and pick up the fold of the other piece. Continue in this way, making the stitches at right angles to the folds and drawing them up so that the two folded edges are joined invisibly.

Small Gifts—Tissue Holder, Spectacle Cleaner and Chatelaine (pages 68-72)

Roses Evening Bag (page 52)

Wattle Brooch and Bag (page 67)

Carnation Spray (page 42)

18

Sewing on Beads

Bring the needle out where the bead is to be sewn, thread the bead, position it on the fabric and take the needle down close to the bead and under the bead, coming up where the next bead is required. If sewing on a single bead in an isolated position, sew through the bead twice before fastening off.

Spider's Web

1. Using a firm thread work a fly stitch, then add a straight stitch each side of the fly stitch into a central point.

2. Bring the thread or ribbon through at the centre and weave it over and under the spokes until the web is filled.

When using ribbon, weave it fairly loosely and let it twist occasionally—the result is a rose-like circle.

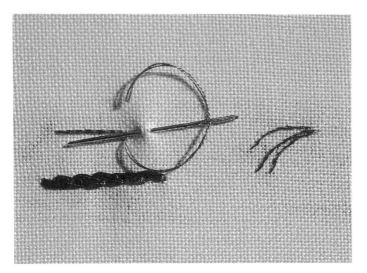

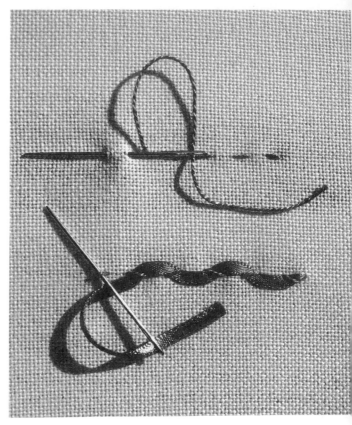

Stem Stitch *(above)*

This can be worked as a fine line or in rows to form a filling.

Threaded Running Stitch *(right)*

Work a row of running stitch, then thread in and out of the running stitch with a ribbon or thread.

Flowers

Carnation

1. Using sewing cotton whip over one edge of the ribbon with fairly small stitches and gather up.

2. For a full flower sew one end of the gathered ribbon to the fabric, in the centre of the flower, then coil the gathered ribbon around this until the flower is full enough. Sew down as invisibly as possible.

3. For a flower in profile work two rows of gathered ribbon, starting with the top row. It is best to work two separate rows, one over the other. Turn in the raw edges and sew neatly to the fabric, sewing the row into place as well.

Making a carnation

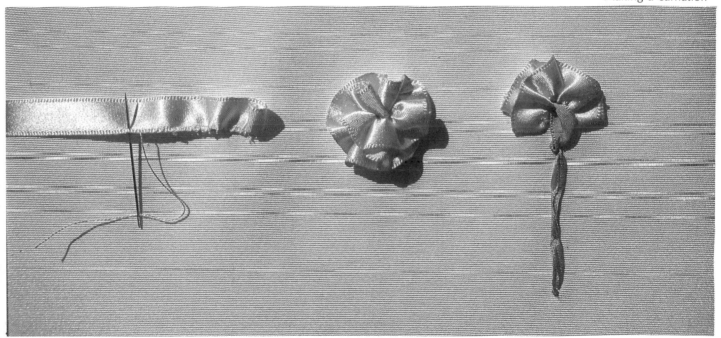

Chrysanthemum

It is best to use soft ribbon for this flower. A stiff ribbon does not hold the twist well. For learning the technique, the nylon strip sold for knitting and crochet is excellent. Small delicate flowers can be worked in silk ribbon. See illustration. Use a short length of ribbon, about 15 cm.

1. Bring the ribbon through the fabric and twist in a clockwise direction—Figure 1 (see next page).

2. Hold the twisted ribbon down with one thumb at the length required for the petal, make a loose loop with the other hand and slip it under the thumb—Figure 2.

3. Put the needle into the fabric in the centre of the loop and pull through to the back until you have a neat curl—Figure 3.

Note: Twisting the ribbon in a clockwise direction will give a curl to the right. If a left-hand curl is required twist anti-clockwise.

Leave the twisted ribbon fairly loose above where it is held down to give a nice curve to the petal.

The curls need to be sewn down, one or two stitches in sewing cotton is enough.

21

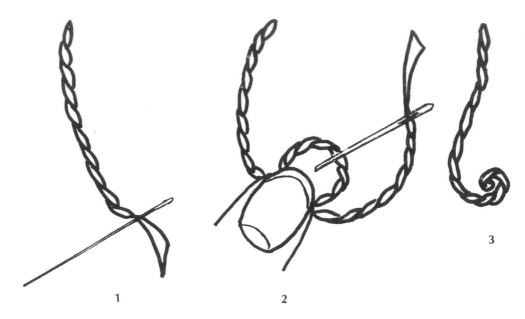

1   2   3

Each petal should be cut off at the back of the work and the end sewn down. This can be done after working several petals.

To achieve a well shaped flower, mark an oval of dots in pencil the size required. Mark the centre of the flower with a dot.

Centres can be worked in loose straight stitches, loops of ribbon or French knots. The addition of some small beads gives an extra sparkle.

Finished chrysanthemums are illustrated on page 56.

Folded Rose

Have a needle threaded with matching cotton. Use 1.5 cm ribbon or wider until you are familiar with the method. If you have a long length of ribbon, do not cut it.

1. Make a fold about 25 cm from one end, as illustrated in the top left of the photograph.

2. Fold right side over the left (top centre).

3. Fold lower end up (top right).

4. Repeat 2 and 3 until you come to the end of the short length of ribbon. There should be about twenty folds.

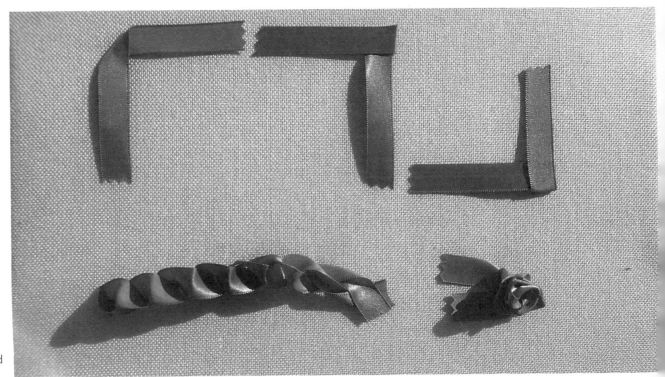

Making a folded rose

5. Hold ends firmly in one hand and release folds (bottom left) and then pull the larger end of ribbon with the other hand, slowly until the rose forms (bottom right).

6. Stitch the rose through the centre once or twice, and through the petals, as invisibly as possible. This will secure it.

7. Cut the ends, fold back neatly and sew onto the fabric.

Fuchsia

1. Using soft ribbon bring three loops through the fabric as illustrated.

2. Stitch through each loop with a small stitch. Do not pull the loop tightly.

3. With satin ribbon wider than the soft ribbon, work four straight stitches as shown. Always come through the fabric outside the flower and make each stitch with a twist, leaving it rather loose.

4. Stitch these petals with sewing cotton as invisibly as possible.

5. Add stamens in two strands of stranded cotton, using a long tailed French knot.

The stamens must appear to come from a central point at the base of the flower.

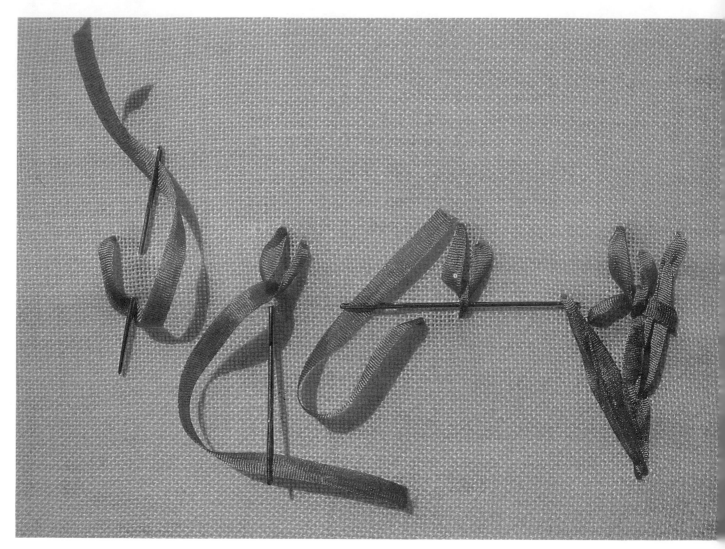

Iris

Soft ribbon is best for this flower.

1. Make an uneven ended chain stitch.

2. Bring the needle out to the left of the chain and below it.

3. Pass the ribbon through the stitch at the end of the chain.

4. Put the needle into the fabric to the right on the same level as the left side.

5. Add another straight stitch between this. Keep all the stitches rather loose, so that the ribbon fluffs out well.

Stems and leaves can be worked in straight stitches in soft silk ribbon.

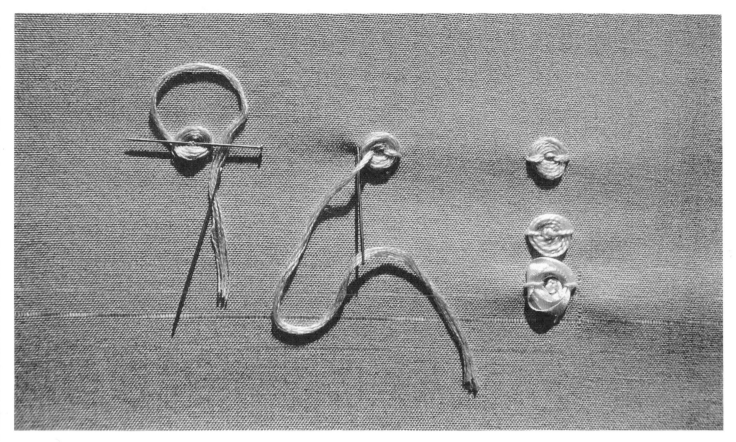

Pin Roses (above)

Put a pin through the fabric where the rose is to be worked, taking up as little of the fabric as possible. Bring the thread through at this point and wind it around the pin several times until the required size is achieved. Take the thread to the back just underneath the last coil. Make a small stitch over all the coils, at each side.

The example shows a pin rose being worked with six strands of stranded cotton. There are also examples worked in Perle cotton number 8 and 3 mm silk ribbon. These have a French knot worked at the centre.

Rolled Rosebud

Have a needle threaded with matching cotton.

1. Make a tight roll on one end of the ribbon, stitch at the end.

2. Fold the ribbon as illustrated and turn around the centre roll. Keep the ribbon out and towards the top of the roll, not tightly against the roll, stitch again.

3. Fold again and turn, stitching at the base.

4. Cut the ribbon straight across and fold over to make a point. Take this around the rose and stitch firmly.

These roses will sit flat on the fabric, not standing up. They look well in a small group or among other flowers.

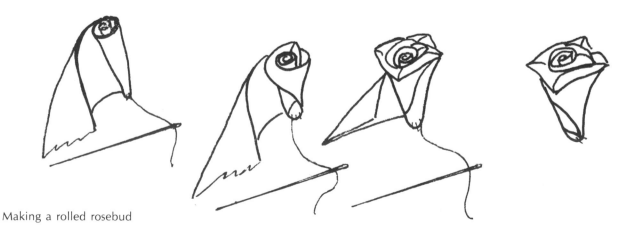

Making a rolled rosebud

Wound Rose

1. Make a loose knot in one end of the ribbon 1 cm from the end. Sew this end to the fabric where the centre of the flower is to be.

2. Fold over and pin to the fabric with a long needle.

3. Wind the ribbon around the needle, twisting the ribbon occasionally, until there is enough for a full rose. Do not pull the ribbon tightly around the needle, but keep it fairly loose, especially at the centre turns.

4. With sewing cotton, sew the ribbon as invisibly as possible in strategic places so that it will hold together.

5. Remove the needle and if necessary add more stitching. Some ribbons are rather stiff and do not wind around the needle easily; they may need to be stitched as you wind.

Ruched Ribbon

Running stitch is worked in zig-zag along the ribbon and then drawn up.

The resulting flexible braid can be used in a number of ways. Examples can be found throughout the book.

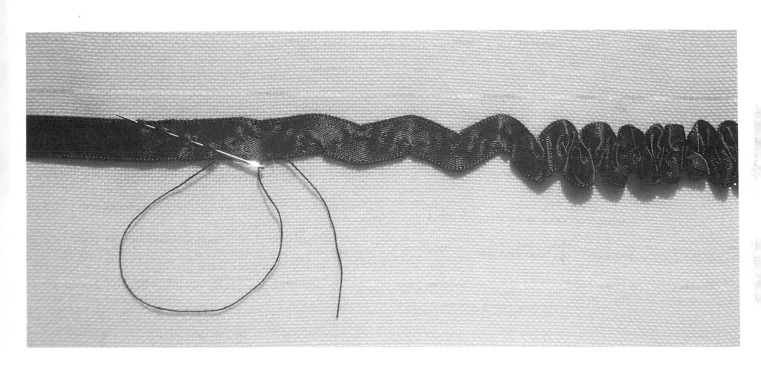

Pictures

Seasons Remembered

These embroideries are a nostalgic remembrance of the seasons of my childhood in England. They are not specific places, but scenes from the mind's eye, romantic and evocative.

The four embroideries that make the set are all worked on dyed fabric. The dye used is one sold for screen printing on fabric; the colours mix together and are easily diluted with water. The dye is set with a hot iron.

In all the pieces the dye has been applied with a fairly large artist's paintbrush to wet fabric, letting the colours blend into one another to give a very soft effect.

When using dye on fabric as the basis for an embroidery, avoid the tendency to paint a picture. Only the suggestion of the background is necessary.

The four pieces are all mounted with velvet mounts and framed in 1930s vintage frames which were repainted to suit each piece.

Spring

Size (embroidery only) 12 cm X 15 cm approx.
The subject is a bluebell wood, looking out to a landscape of hills. I wanted to capture the fresh yellow green of new beech leaves and the hazy blue of the bluebells.

The cotton fabric was painted with dye in blues and yellow greens to suggest the areas of sky, trees and bluebells.

The hills were worked first in lines of stem stitch in one strand of stranded cotton. A hedge was suggested by ruched silk ribbon in a dark yellow green (see illustration of ruched ribbon on previous page).

Satin ribbon and some fine rayon braid were stitched down over the landscape to start the tree trunks. These were stitched over with cretan stitch and straight stitches in one strand of stranded cotton in several shades of greys and soft fawn. The ends of the braid were deliberately frayed and stitched down. Straight stitches in green silk ribbon, worked horizontally, were the basis for the leafy tree tops and straight stitches in satin and silk ribbons worked vertically for the bluebells.

The blue stitches were made shorter as they went into the hills, to suggest distance. The areas of foliage and bluebells were then stitched all over in cretan stitch, using one strand of stranded cotton and working the stitch horizontally for the foliage and vertically for the bluebells.

Many shades of green, yellow and blue were used, with brighter colours to the front of the picture.

Using many tones of colour will always give a rich effect, and the contrast of dull and shiny materials adds to this effect. Note that the stitchery is deliberately uneven, making the soft texture required.

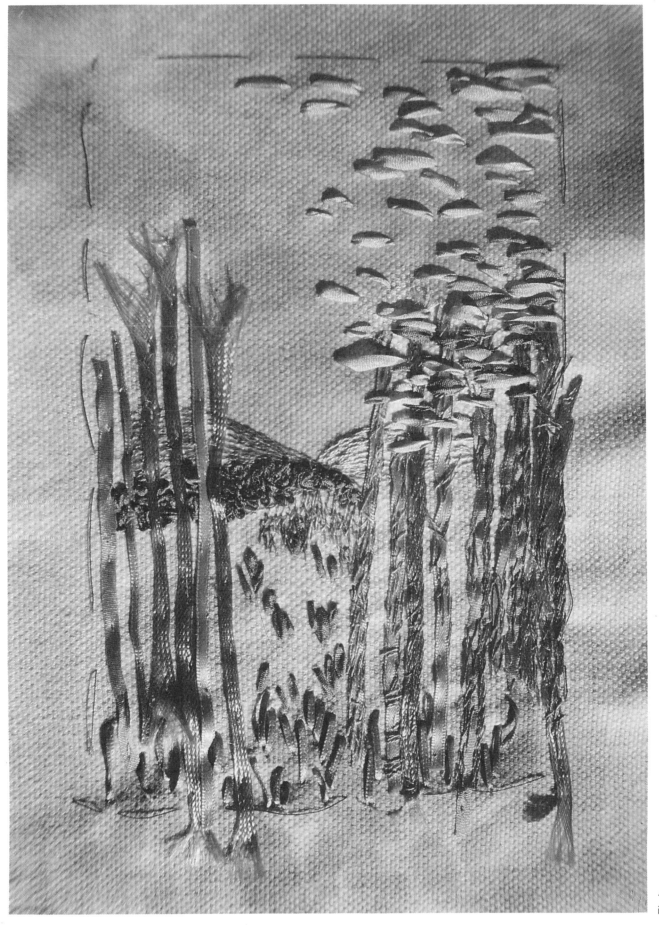

'Spring'—work
in progress

'Spring'—
finished but
unmounted

30

Summer

Size (embroidery only) 18 cm × 14 cm approx.
The scene is part of a public park, with lawns, avenues of trees, a lake and beds of flowers.

The cotton calico was dyed as before, ruched ribbon was sewn in a line to suggest bushes and manipulated into fan shapes for small trees. The ribbon was stitched down and then embroidered over with French knots and chain stitches.

Short pieces of dark green ribbon were sewn down horizontally where the conifers were to be and these were stitched over with several shades of cotton using cretan stitch worked horizontally. Some long straight stitches were added last to give direction to the trees.

The lake was worked with a shaded knitting ribbon stitched down as invisibly as possible and then broken lines of stem stitch in fine thread added.

The flower beds in the foreground were suggested by a gathered length of striped gauze ribbon, stitched over with bullion knots in reds and fly stitch in greens in Perle cotton number 8.

There are also chain stitches in green silk ribbon and French knots in various threads in bright pinks.

The overhanging tree is worked in single chain stitches in ribbons and various threads in copper colours.

The mount is light blue velvet.

Autumn

Size (embroidery only) 12 cm X 14 cm approx.

What I wanted to convey in this piece was a garden, rich with the colours of dahlias, dead leaves, woody stalks, shrubs turning colour and some bare trees.

The trees in the background were worked first, on dyed calico. Many shades of grey and soft pink in fine silk and one strand of stranded cotton were used in fly stitch and cretan stitch, worked very unevenly, with the colours overlapping and in directions to form a tree shape.

Under these trees several rows of a shaded knitted ribbon were sewn down and stitched over with long detached chain stitches in 2 strands and 1 strand of stranded cotton, in colours similar to but darker than the trees.

The top part of the flower bed is composed of ruched shaded knitting ribbon, sewn down with fly stitches and French knots added into it in similar colours and a golden yellow.

Straight stitches in various ribbons in mauves, reds, and apricot form the background for feather stitch and fly stitch in similar colours and deeper tones in threads of various thickness.

French knots in several shades of golden yellow have been added at the edge of this area.

The foreground is composed of running stitches in Perle cotton number 5, threaded with silk ribbon in a circular direction, the colours varying from dark red to bright pink.

French knots in satin ribbon, handspun silk and Perle cotton number 5 are worked among ribbons.

A flat area of shaded ribbon, sewn down with patches of cretan stitch, forms the lower edge. On the right hand side, there is a small section of green silk ribbon in single chains, overlaid with chains in golden yellow fine thread.

The mount is dusty pink velvet.

Winter

Size (embroidery only) 20 cm × 15 cm approx.

This is a snow scene in the country, just before dusk, when the light sometimes has a pink tinge and there is the threat of more snow.

The cotton fabric was dyed mauve grey and pink, leaving most of the foreground undyed to give the impression of snow.

The line of the hills in the distance was worked first, in stem stitch with fine silk thread in a soft grey.

The trees in the background were worked in straight stitches and fly stitches in ribbon and threads in greys and soft browns.

The line of trees in the middle distance have silk and satin ribbons as the basis of the trunks, stitched over with Perle cotton number 5 and stranded cotton in greys and browns, using straight stitches.

The hedge has a background of cross stitches in soft ribbon with overlaid stitches in Perle cotton number 8 and stranded cotton.

The gate is worked with stranded cotton in long stitches caught down with sewing cotton.

The tracks to the gate are running stitches in fawn stranded cotton.

The plant forms in the foreground are straight and fly stitches in satin ribbon, Perle cotton number 5 and stranded cotton.

'Winter' has a grey velvet mount.

Florist's Window (cover)

The floor and shelf areas have been covered with dull grey-green taffeta, bonded to the linen background with fusible web. The details have been machine stitched, including the basket which is machined in rows of an automatic pattern. The flower containers are of black non-woven interfacing, black satin and green cotton. These fabrics have had fusible web bonded to them, been cut into the required shapes, then bonded to the background and machine stitched around the edges.

Bonding fabrics together with fusible web is a very easy form of applique and gives a very neat and clean outline.

The flowers in each container have been treated differently and make use of ribbons and hand stitchery. Some are ruched ribbon, some chain stitches, some loops of ribbon, others are cretan stitch, straight stitches or fly stitches. The shades of colour and contrast of dull and shiny materials give the work richness and depth.

'Seasons Remembered' (pages 28–33)

Spring

Summer

Autumn

These pictures are all mounted in velvet and framed in restored frames of 1930s vintage

Winter

'Jibbon Beach' (page 39)

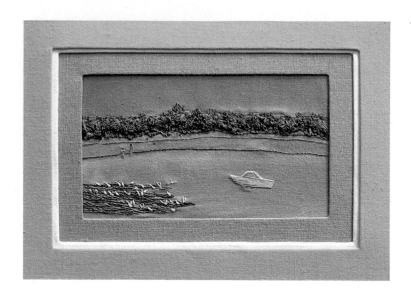

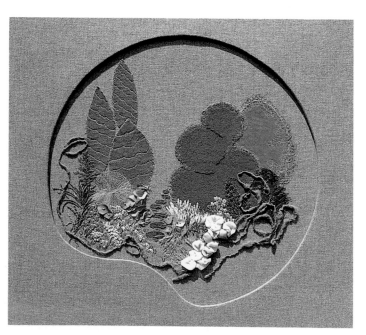

'Autumn in Bright, Victoria' by Doris Waltho (page 40)

'Yellow Garden' by Kath Chate (page 41)

36

Butterflies and Flowers (page 46)

Fuchsia Trail (page 45)

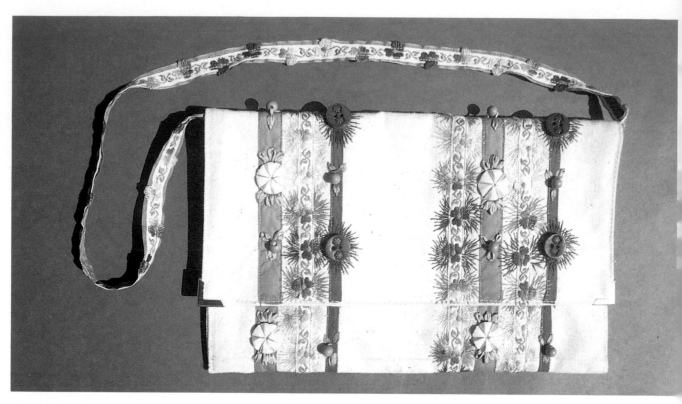

Floral Stripe Handbag (page 58)

Bows and Garlands (page 48)

Jibbon Beach

Size (embroidery only) 20 cm × 15 cm

Jibbon Beach is in Sydney, Australia and is portrayed on a summer day. The colours of the sky, water, sand and foliage have been intensified to give the impression of strong light.

Washes of blue and yellow dye were painted on to wet cotton fabric to define the areas of sea, sand and sky. The strip of coastal area was worked first with various ribbons, folded and ruched then stitched to the fabric.

Cretan stitch in a variety of threads was worked irregularly into and around the ribbons.

A line of stem stitch defines the edge of the sand and the tide line; the figures on the beach were worked in straight stitches.

The boat was cut out of non-woven interfacing and the details drawn on it in pencil. It was stitched down with long stitches which give the effect of shadow.

Golden yellow silk ribbon and narrow braid were laid in long straight stitches to start the rocky area. This was stitched over with stem stitch in Perle cotton.

The flying seagulls are fly stitches in white Perle cotton and the static gulls are single twisted chain stitches.

The embroidery is mounted in a series of 4 fabric covered mounts of different widths in the colours of sand, sky, birds and trees. The proportion of each colour in the mounts is roughly the same as in the embroidery, highlighting and accentuating the colours of the beach scene.

Detail from 'Autumn in Bright, Victoria'

Autumn in Bright, Victoria (Doris Waltho)

Embroidery size 33 cm × 20 cm; total size 48 cm × 36 cm
This colourful picture is a beautiful blend of applied fabrics, dyeing and hand stitchery in both ribbons and threads in great variety.

The basic fabric is calico, dyed to define the areas of path and trees. The dye was applied to wet fabric to get a very soft effect.

The area of the trees was overlaid with pieces of sheer cotton and organza to strengthen the colours. The tree tops were then stitched over with running stitches in silk ribbons, some satin ribbon, and many different threads, from quite heavy handspun silk thread to very fine stranded silk or cotton. The direction of the stitches and the range of colour, from dark wine red to pale apricot and lime green, gives the impression of autumn leaves.

The tree trunks are velvet ribbon, with raised stem band worked along one edge, the other edge sewn with either back stitch or stem stitch.

Stem stitch also forms the pathway, in fine silk threads and stranded cotton in shades of cream, white and grey. Note how many shades are used, with the stronger colour to the foreground to give the work perspective. The areas of fallen leaves are worked in running stitch with stranded cottons and silks in similar colours to the leaves of the trees, but the lighter texture gives this area good definition.

The work has been framed with a triple mount. The yellow, tan and fawn mount boards add to the colour effect and the touch of gold on the wood frame gives a pleasing finish.

Detail from 'Yellow Garden' showing flowers and stitchery

The Yellow Garden (Kath Chate)

Size 62 cm × 70 cm (including the mount)

The garden scene depicted combines applique with machine and hand embroidery in ribbons and threads. It is worked on a wool fabric and the applied materials include velvet, wool, silk, cotton and voile. The simple shapes of the trees and shrubs in the background are applied with freely worked machine embroidery. The tones of green blend with the wool ground, and are not too dominating, giving the effect of distance. A path is suggested by ovals of wool fabric stitched by hand with wool thread.

Of the two groups of flower shapes in fabric, one consists of bonded silks and cottons cut into irregular hexagons and sewn down in the centre with groups of small French knots. The other, paler flowers are circles of voile and silk gathered around the edge and pulled up, then turned over and sewn down with a large French knot at the centre.

Both these groups of flowers are rather three dimensional and stand well away from the background.

The delightful hand stitchery is a very good example of the use of simple stitches in a variety of materials.

Fly, stem, chain, cretan and straight stitches are worked in satin and silk ribbons, crewel wool and Perle cotton. The crewel wool stitchery softens the effect of the shiny satin ribbons, achieving a subtle blend of colour and texture.

The line of continuous couching in heavy handspun wool suggests more shrubs and clumps of plants at the lower edge of the picture. The movement of this line is echoed by the unusually shaped mount which draws the eye into the focal area of yellow flowers.

Designs for Clothing

Carnation Spray

This design was originally worked on the very full sleeves of an evening blouse of wool crepe. It would be equally suitable embroidered on a skirt, pocket, jacket or jumper. The quantities quoted are for one motif only.

You will need:

1. 1 metre each of 10 mm velvet ribbon and 10 mm satin ribbon to match. Sewing thread to match these ribbons.
2. 1 metre each of 20 mm gauze ribbon and 35 mm shaded gauze ribbon, in similar colours. (Satin or nylon ribbon may be substituted.)
3. 1 metre of 1.5 mm satin ribbon in another colour.
4. 1 metre narrow gold braid or satin ribbon. Sewing cotton to match.
5. 2 metres silk or soft polyester ribbon in a colour to tone with the wider ribbons.
6. Stranded cotton in a darker shade of the 1.5 mm ribbon and in a lighter shade of the background colour.
7. Beads in a light bright colour to tone with the wider ribbons.

Method:

1. Mark on the fabric, with either a water soluble pen or basting thread, the centres of the carnations, the lines of the sprays of flowers and the stems.

2. With 20 mm ribbon make 1 full carnation, 1 profile flower and 1 bud.

3. Fold the 35 mm ribbon almost in half and make 1 full carnation, 1 profile flower and 1 bud.

4. Sew these flowers in place as invisibly as possible, adding twisted chain stitches in silk ribbon at the base of the profile flowers and buds.

5. Sew the gold braid or ribbon along the stem lines with matching sewing cotton.

6. Work the larger sprays of flowers in 1.5 mm satin ribbon with 5 single chains in a circle for each flower. Work another chain in 6 strands of stranded cotton inside the ribbon chains. The buds at the ends of the sprays are single chains in ribbon with chains in stranded cotton outside them.

7. Work stems to these sprays in whipped chain stitch, using 4 strands of stranded cotton.

8. Sew a bead in the centre of each flower.

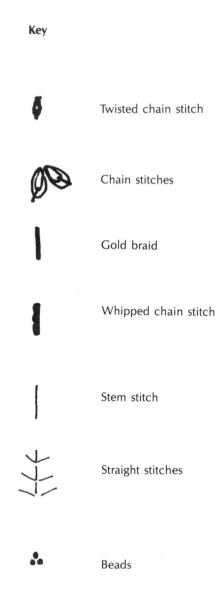

Key

Twisted chain stitch

Chain stitches

Gold braid

Whipped chain stitch

Stem stitch

Straight stitches

Beads

See instructions on page 21 for carnation flowers

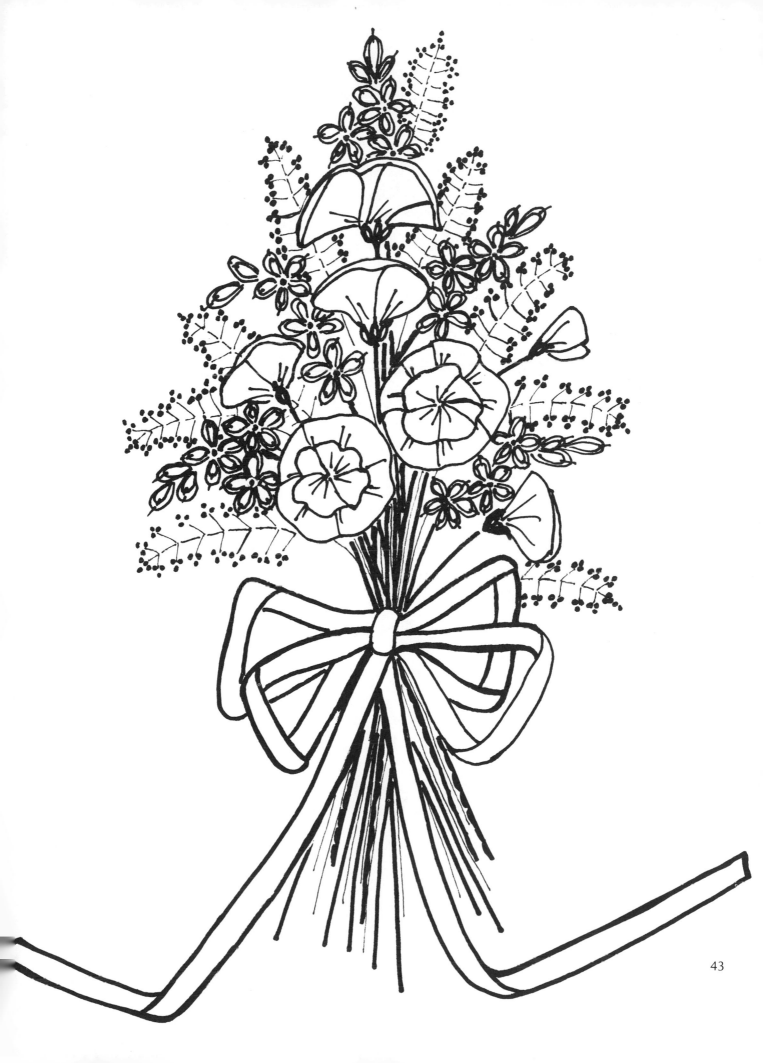

9. Using one strand of cotton work the beaded sprays. Start at the top of the spray and sew 3 or 4 beads close together, *make a straight stitch directly underneath them. Take the needle out to the left about 3 mm and sew on 3 beads, then make a straight stitch from the beads to the centre. Repeat to the right then repeat from * until the spray is completed.

10. Work stems in one strand of cotton in stem stitch.

11. Stitch the satin ribbon to the back of the velvet ribbon with a small zig-zag stitch on the sewing machine, sewing along each edge.

12. Cut 0.5 metre of this prepared ribbon and tie a bow in the centre. Fold the two ends under the knot to form a double bow, and sew to the centre of the knot.

13. Fold the rest of the ribbon in half and sew the fold to the back of bow at the knot.

14. Pin the bow in place over the stems of the design, pin out the ribbon similarly to the illustration, and sew down with matching thread.

Fuchsia Trail

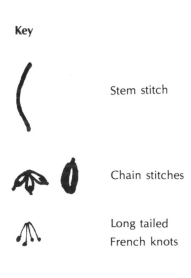

Key

Stem stitch

Chain stitches

Long tailed
French knots

See page 23
for instructions
for fuchsias

Fuchsia Trail

This design was worked each side of the yoke of a dressing gown. Because the knit velour fabric of the garment is very difficult to pull ribbon through, the embroidery was worked on a wide velvet ribbon, then applied to the yoke of the gown.

The design would also look well on a blouse or jumper, perhaps on one side only.

Quantities are quoted for one trail only, approximately 28 cm long. You will need:

1. 1 metre each of 2 shades of 4 mm satin ribbon.
2. 2 metres of 3 mm silk or soft polyester ribbon in a contrast colour.
3. 1 metre of two other shades of silk or soft polyester ribbon.
4. 1 metre of 1.5 mm satin ribbon in another colour.
5. Stranded cotton in a dark shade to tone with the garment.
6. Perle cotton number 8 in a lighter shade to tone with the garment.
7. Stranded cotton in a lighter shade to tone with the 4 mm ribbon.
8. 1 metre of 5 mm velvet ribbon, if working on this is preferred.

Method:

1. Transfer the curving line of the design to the cut out yoke of the garment or the wide velvet ribbon with either a water soluble fabric marking pen or basting.

2. Mark with a dot the placement of the flowers and buds.

3. Using 6 strands of stranded cotton work the curving line in stem stitch.

4. Work fuchsias in the silk or polyester ribbons and satin ribbons. See instructions on page 23.

5. Work half open flowers, making 3 straight stitches close together in silk or polyester ribbon with 3 stitches over them in 1.5 mm satin ribbon, and a small straight stitch at the top of the flowers.

6. Work buds in silk or polyester ribbon, making two straight stitches almost on top of one another and a very small straight stitch at the top.

7. Work groups of leaves in Perle cotton number 8 in single chains.

If the design is worked on wide ribbon, it can be applied to the yoke with a machine stitch as illustrated or hand sewn. If hand sewing, sew down with a stem stitch in matching thread on both edges.

Detail of Fuchsia Trail

Butterflies and Flowers

The butterflies in this design have been made on the sewing machine, and the flowers are hand embroidered.

This is a rather free design that could be interpreted in a number of ways and adapted to suit individual requirements. The method of working the butterflies and the flower spikes is described and illustrated, but the assembling of these elements to form a design is left to the individual.

The illustration has been worked on polyester jersey across the shoulder and neckline of a short sleeved top.

Key

Machine satin stitch

Whipped chain stitch

Cut out holes

Beads

Rosette chain stitch

Twisted chain stitch

Detached chain stitch

Top decorated with Flowers and Butterflies

Butterflies

You will need:

1. For 3 or 4 butterflies, a piece of satin 23 cm square.
2. A piece of cotton in a toning colour the same size.
3. A piece of fusible web the same size.
4. Shaded machine embroidery cotton to tone with the satin.
5. Crystal beads (5 for each butterfly).

Method:

1. Bond the satin and cotton together with the fusible web, carefully following the instructions with the latter.

2. Transfer the design of the butterflies to the bonded fabric, having the centre of each butterfly on the straight grain of the fabric.

3. Using the shaded machine embroidery cotton, satin stitch by machine around the outlines of the butterflies.

4. Cut out the butterflies as close as possible to the satin stitch, taking care not to cut the stitching. If this does happen, place the butterfly in a piece of typing paper and satin stitch over the edge again, then tear the paper away.

5. Sew the butterflies in place on the embroidery by hand, using the machine embroidery cotton and sewing in strategic places over the satin stitch.

6. Sew the crystal beads down the body of the butterfly through the background fabric.

Flowers

You will need:

1. 3 mm silk or soft polyester ribbon in 3 colours—5 metres of each would be enough for a top similar to the one illustrated.
2. Stranded cotton for stems.
3. Stranded cotton in lighter or darker shades of the colours of the ribbons.
4. Small round beads for flower centres.

Method:

1. Work each flower with 6 single rosette chain stitches in silk or polyester ribbon. Over these stitches work a single chain stitch in one strand of stranded cotton, catching the end of the rosette chain to hold it. Work buds at top of spikes in twisted chain stitch.

2. Sew a bead in the centre of each flower.

3. Work stems in whipped chain stitch.

Bows and Garlands

Ribbon embroidery can be used very effectively in lingerie as shown by the nightdress yoke illustrated. When working on a sheer or very light coloured fabric take care that the ends of ribbons and threads are finished off so that they do not show through the fabric.

The design illustrated is worked on cotton voile. The quantities quoted are for the design as illustrated. The diagram is of the bow and garland only. The arrangement of these elements is left to the individual.

You will need:

1. 2 metres of 2 close shades of 3 mm silk or soft polyester ribbon.
2. Stranded cotton to match the darker shade. Perle cotton number 8 to match the lighter shade.
3. Stranded cotton in 3 shades of a contrast colour, and to match the fabric.

Method:

1. Take 0.5 metre of each of the 2 shades of silk or polyester ribbon and tie a bow, using the 2 ribbons together.
2. Pin the double bow in place where required, pin out all parts, then baste.
3. Work stem stitch in one strand of stranded cotton along the edges of the darker ribbon.

4. Work French knots in Perle cotton number 8 down the centre of the lighter ribbon.
5. If using several bows in the design, make them and embroider in place.
6. With a sharp pencil mark a series of dots on the fabric along the centre line of the garland, between the bows.
7. Starting at the centre of the garland and using the deepest shade of the contrasting stranded cotton, work 3 pin roses—the centre rose should be slightly larger than the others. Follow with one each side of these in the next shade, then 2 each side in the lightest shade. Work a French knot in the centre of each rose in Perle cotton.
8. Using the two lighter shades of the roses work the rest of the garland in French knots, starting with 6 strands and graduating to 3 strands. Add French knots between the pin roses to fill out the garland.

Seams in sheer fabric should be narrowly trimmed and overcast, by hand or machine, or French seamed.

The illustrated yoke has a line of French knots just inside the neckline and yoke, at the edge of the trimmed seam. This makes an attractive finish.

Key

 Ribbons

 Pin roses

 French knots

Green Daisies (Kath Chate)

The embroidery on this jumper is worked over one shoulder and sleeve, both front and back.

The daisies are grouped very irregularly, no two groups quite the same, and are linked with continuous looping and curving lines.

Two shades of silk ribbon have been used for the daisies which are worked in long detached chains, six to each flower. These stitches are worked over with a line of twisted chain stitch in a shiny thread in a similar colour to the ribbon.

The centres of the flowers are bullion knots worked in silk threads in colours to blend with the flowers. The continuous couched lines that link the groups of daisies are worked in either handspun silk or wool thread. The irregularities of the thread make a more interesting line than a smooth thread.

The colour of these lines is very close to that of the knitted jumper and does not make too great a contrast.

The illustration is of one group of daisies only. This type of design would not be difficult to work up and different flower forms could be used.

Detail of Green Daisies design

Key

Chain stitch

Twisted chain stitch

Bullion knots

Couching

Bags and Accessories

Roses Evening Bag and Hair Slide

The evening bag illustrated has a 1920s vintage frame and handle, and the design of the embroidery is related to the shape of the handle.

It is important when making a bag to consider any special use for it, and to include the handles in the design.

The fabric used for the bag illustrated is a polyester moire taffeta.

This design could also be adapted for a box top or for evening wear.

Wound rose   Ribbon loop   Spider's web   French knot   Beads

Evening Bag

For a bag with a design of the size in the diagram you will need:

1. A piece of fabric 20 cm × 40 cm.
2. A piece of lining and a piece of thin wadding the same size.
3. 0.5 metre of 15 mm satin ribbon in a colour to tone with the fabric.
4. 1 metre of 10 mm satin ribbon in a lighter shade.
5. 1 metre of 10 mm velvet ribbon to match the fabric.
6. 1.5 metre of 3 mm silk or polyester ribbon in a contrast colour.
7. Sewing cotton to match the ribbons and fabric.
8. Perle cotton number 8 in a similar tone to the velvet ribbon.
9. Small silver or gold beads.

Method:

1. Mark the lines of the edge of the design on the fabric with a water soluble fabric marking pen or a line of basting. Mark the placement of the 3 roses.

2. Make a wound rose in the centre of the design in the 15 mm satin ribbon. See illustration on page 26. Sew beads in the centre.

3. Make two wound roses in the 10 mm satin ribbon each side of the centre. Sew beads in the centre.

4. With the velvet ribbon, make two bunches of 3 loops approximately 4 cm long. Sew the ends together, then place them just under the edge of the central rose and sew in place, sewing the loops here and there as invisibly as possible. Make two single loops and sew at the tops of the outer roses.

5. Work spider's webs in Perle cotton number 8.

6. Work French knots around the spider's webs in the silk or polyester ribbon.

7. Start the beading at the edges of the design. Attach each bead with a back stitch (see diagram on page 19). Continue beading in rows in brick fashion until the ground of the design is completely covered.

8. Line and interline the bag with the thin wadding and lining.

9. Most bag mounts and handles have holes in them along the edges and the bag can be attached to the mount through these. Use strong thread to match the bag and use a running stitch through the bag and holes. When this is completed, sew back to the start in between the previous stitches. Ribbon can be threaded through these stitches to make an attractive finish.

Hairslide

For the hairslide you will need:

1. 1 hairslide about 8 cm long.
2. 1 piece of firm plastic 9 cm × 6 cm (plastic from an ice cream carton is ideal).
3. Piece of fabric about 20 cm × 8 cm.
4. 0.5 metre 15 mm satin ribbon.
5. 0.5 metre 1.5 mm satin ribbon in a light colour.
6. 0.5 metre 3 mm silk or polyester ribbon in another colour.
7. 0.5 metre 10 mm velvet ribbon.
8. Small silver or gold beads.

Method:

1. Work a wound rose in the centre of half the fabric, sew beads in the centre.

2. Make two bunches of velvet ribbon loops as for the bag and attach each side of the rose.

3. Add French knots in the 1.5 mm satin ribbon or silk or polyester ribbon.

4. Bead the ground as for the bag.

5. Cut the plastic in an oval shape large enough to cover the hairslide.

6. Centre the embroidery over the plastic and run a gathering thread around it. Pull up firmly and fasten off.

7. Line the back with the same fabric, turning the edges under and sewing neatly.

8. Attach the hairslide to the back of the mounted embroidery, sewing it firmly where possible.

Roses Hairslide

Back of hairslide

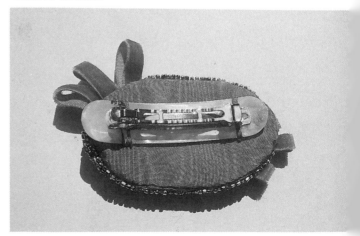

Flower Basket Bag by
Doris Waltho (page 62)

Haircombs (page 57)

Left below: Beads (page 60)

Waratah Brooch and Bag (page 65)

Green Daisies by Kath Chate (page 50)

Pendant and Bag (page 63)

Chrysanthemum Brooch and Bag (page 64)

Haircombs

Haircombs are a fashion accessory that can be decorated in a number of ways for day or evening wear. Bows, flowers, folded and ruched ribbon are all effective and could be used in endless permutations. The two combs illustrated are both very simple to make.

For the comb with 3 roses you will need:

1. 1 haircomb.
2. 0.75 metre of 22 mm satin ribbon.
3. 0.5 metre of 35 mm satin ribbon.
4. 0.5 metre of 15 mm satin ribbon (choose 3 tones of one colour).
5. Sewing cotton to match the ribbons.
6. 3 diamante beads.

Method:

1. Cut a piece of the 22 mm ribbon twice the width of the comb plus 2 cm.

2. Fold 1 cm of this ribbon to the back of one end of the top of the comb, then sew the ribbon to the outside of the comb through the prongs. Take care not to extend the ribbon down the prongs. If there is any surplus width of ribbon leave it at the top of the comb.

3. Make 3 folded roses with the three different ribbons, leaving tails on the two smaller ones.

4. Sew a diamante bead to each flower.

5. Sew the roses to the comb through the ribbon.

6. Fold the other half of the ribbon attached to the comb to the back, turn in the cut edge and sew neatly together at both edges.

For the comb with rosebuds and pearls you will need:

1. 1 haircomb
2. 20 cm of 15 mm velvet ribbon.
3. 0.5 metre of 15 mm satin ribbon.
4. 0.5 metre of 3 mm satin ribbon with a picot edge.
5. 15 cm each of 20 mm and 25 cm satin ribbon in two colours.
6. About 16 pearls, preferably in graduated sizes.

Method:

1. Attach the velvet ribbon to the comb in the way described for the other comb.

2. Fold the picot edged ribbon into two bunches of loops of different lengths. Sew the ends together. Sew these to the comb through the velvet ribbon.

3. Make 5 rolled rosebuds, 3 in the 15 mm satin ribbon and one each in the other ribbons. Sew these to the comb over the bunches of loops.

4. Sew the pearls to the comb.

5. Fold the rest of the velvet ribbon to the back of the comb, turn in the end and sew neatly down both edges of the ribbon.

Floral Stripe Handbag

This design combines floral braid, ribbons, wooden beads, leather buttons and stitchery.

There are many beautiful floral braids available and variations on this striped design would not be difficult to work out.

The braid used in the illustration has been integrated with the ribbons by means of the stitchery around each flower. The gradation of colour in the threads makes a more interesting effect than if only one colour were used. Tote bags, cushions and clothing could also be embroidered in a similar way.

The handbag illustrated measures 26.5 cm × 17 cm.

The embroidery was worked in a continuous strip on the front, back and flap.

The fabric is a lightweight canvas, lined with a cotton to match one of the ribbons in the embroidery.

For a handbag this size you will need:

1. A piece of lightweight canvas or heavy cotton 70 cm × 30 cm.
2. A piece of cotton for lining 35 cm × 30 cm.
3. 3 metres of floral braid approximately 1.5 cm wide.
4. 3 metres of 15 mm nylon ribbon to tone with one of the colours in the braid.
5. 3 metres of 8 mm nylon ribbon in another colour.
6. Stranded cotton in 3 shades to tone with colours in the braid.
7. 10 × 2 cm diameter flat wooden 'spacer' beads.
8. 12 × 1.5 cm diameter buttons.
9. 3 metres each of 3 mm silk or polyester ribbon in lighter shades of the colours of the nylon ribbons.
10. Sewing cotton to match fabric, braid and ribbons.
11. 2 brass corners (optional).
12. 2 pairs Velcro spots for fastening.

Method:

1. Decide on the spacing of the braid and ribbons and the width of the stripes the embroidery will form.

2. Pin the braids and ribbon to the fabric and machine stitch down both edges with a fairly small stitch. Always stitch in the same direction to avoid buckling the ribbon.

3. Sew on the beads and buttons where required and add simple stitches around them in the silk or polyester ribbon. Single chain stitches have been used on the bag illustrated.

4. With one strand of stranded cotton work cretan stitch around flowers of the braid, carrying the stitch outside the braid and working it unevenly. Graduate the colours of the thread to tone with the colours in the braid.

5. Take 65 cm of the braid and the 15 mm nylon ribbon and machine stitch the braid to the ribbon, down both edges.

6. Machine stitch the lining right sides together to each end of the embroidered fabric, taking 1.5 cm turnings. Trim seams and press towards the lining.

7. Fold the fabric, right sides together, so that the lining section is at one end. The other end, with double canvas fabric, forms the flap of the bag.

8. Insert the prepared handle into the sides just above the lining and pin, making sure it is not twisted—it will be between the layers of fabric.

9. Machine stitch the sides, leaving an opening at the lining end large enough to turn the bag right side out. Trim seams.

10. Turn the bag right side out and press carefully. Make sure the lining does not extend beyond the edge of the bag. Turn the edges of the opening under and press, then slip stitch by hand.

11. Machine stitch along the edge of the end that is lined.

12. Fold this end up to the top of the lining and pin at the sides, then baste.

13. Machine stitch at the edge, down the sides of the bag and around the flap. Use a fairly large stitch.

14. Hand sew the velcro spots in position at each side under the flap and corresponding places on the bag.

15. To attach brass corners to the flap, spread a little fabric glue into the groove of the corner with a needle, slip onto the fabric corner, then cover with a piece of scrap fabric and pinch together with pliers.

Black satin beads and earrings with spider's web roses in satin ribbon and pearls

Beads

Fabric beads are easily made and embroidered. Combined with more conventional beads they make very unusual jewellery.

Three different necklaces are illustrated.

One is of large dark blue velvet beads embroidered in running stitch and threaded running stitch and threaded with crimson and mauve ribbons. These beads are combined with large grey pearl beads.

One is of silk in four bright colours, embroidered with silk ribbons and glass and crystal beads, using chain stitch.

Another is of black satin with spider's web roses worked in cream satin ribbon and pearls.

To make beads you need:

Enough fabric to cut on the bias for the number of beads you require
Wadding
Ribbons
Sewing cotton to match the fabric and ribbons
Beads
Fishing line

Method:

1. Cut a 6 cm wide strip of fabric on the bias.

2. Fold in half, right sides together, and machine stitch, taking in 0.5 cm seam.

3. Trim the seam and turn right side out. This tubing or rouleau is the basis for the beads.

4. Cut into lengths the size of the beads required, allowing an extra 1 cm for turnings. If making a necklace, cut all the bead lengths first, to get them a uniform size.

5. Take a piece of wadding approximately 5 cm × 10 cm and roll it tightly to make a 5 cm long roll.

6. Stuff this into the cut length of rouleau using a stuffing stick or the points of small scissors.

7. Turn in one end of the fabric at the end of the bead, and run a running stitch around it. Pull up firmly and fasten off. Repeat at the other end.

8. Decorate the bead. This is best done after the beads are made. Keep the embroidery as simple as possible. Threads and soft ribbons can be pulled through the ends of the fabric beads to start.

To make a spider's web on a bead, bring the thread for the groundwork through to the place required and work as usual. Thread the ribbon under the groundwork and stitch down. This is easier than pulling the ribbon through the fabric bead. When the web is completed take the ribbon under the groundwork again and sew down.

To thread the beads, take a length of fishing line approximately twice the finished length of the necklace and thread the beads on this. Glass, plastic or wooden beads can be threaded between the fabric beads.

You will need a large darning needle to thread the fabric beads; this will usually have to be unthreaded to thread the ordinary beads as they have a small hole.

If using a fastener, knot the fishing line very tightly several times to each end of the fastener, then thread back through at least two fabric beads before trimming.

Earrings can very easily be made and attached to hooks or clips obtained from craft shops.

Making a
fabric bead

Velvet beads embroidered with running stitch and threaded running stitch, threaded with ribbons and combined with large pearl beads; silk beads embroidered with silk ribbons and glass and crystal beads

Flower Basket Bag (Doris Waltho)

This delightful and unusual bag would make a charming accessory for a bridesmaid or highlight an evening outfit.

The embroidery is simple, comprising wound roses, spider's webs, cross stitches, detached chains and French knots. These are worked in various ribbons and threads, including handspun silk thread, silk, satin and gauze ribbons, knitting ribbon and Perle cotton. The basket is worked in buttonhole stitch in shaded Perle cotton number 5, which is threaded with satin ribbon. The rows of buttonhole stitch are worked in brick fashion with the stitches fairly wide apart. The edges of the satin ribbon have been machine stitched to secure them. Each side of the bag is worked similarly, but not exactly the same, keeping the outside edges alike in shape so that the two halves of the bag will join together well.

The embroidered sides are folded over thin wadding, each lined separately, then the two sides joined together with ladder stitch, leaving an adequate opening. A velcro spot makes a satisfactory fastening, placed in the centre of the opening.

The handle is of plaited ribbons in colours that appear in the embroidery.

Detail of embroidery on the flower basket bag

Pendant and Bag

A pendant with its own matching bag makes a very special gift. This idea is one that can be carried out with other items of fabric jewellery. The bag can be related to the jewellery by the materials, colour, design or combinations of these elements.

The Pendant

You will need:

1. A small piece of silk approx. 9 cm × 10 cm.
2. 1 metre of 3 mm silk or polyester ribbon in 2 colours.
3. Sewing thread to match the fabric.
4. 0.5 metre of 1.5 mm satin ribbon.
5. A piece of card or plastic 9 cm × 10 cm.
6. Small glass beads in 3 or 4 colours to tone with the fabric and ribbons.
7. Stranded cotton to tone with one of the colours of the beads.
8. A chain or enough ribbon to hang the pendant.
9. 3 large beads in a contrast colour.
10. Fabric glue.
11. A piece of suede, felt or thin leather 9 cm × 10 cm.

Method:

1. Mark the central shape on the fabric with pencil dots.

2. At the centre of this shape work a small spider's web in one of the silk ribbons.

3. Bead solidly around the spider's web to the edge of the shape.

4. With the other silk ribbon work a row of small loops around the beaded shape.

5. Attach each loop to the fabric with a bead.

Key

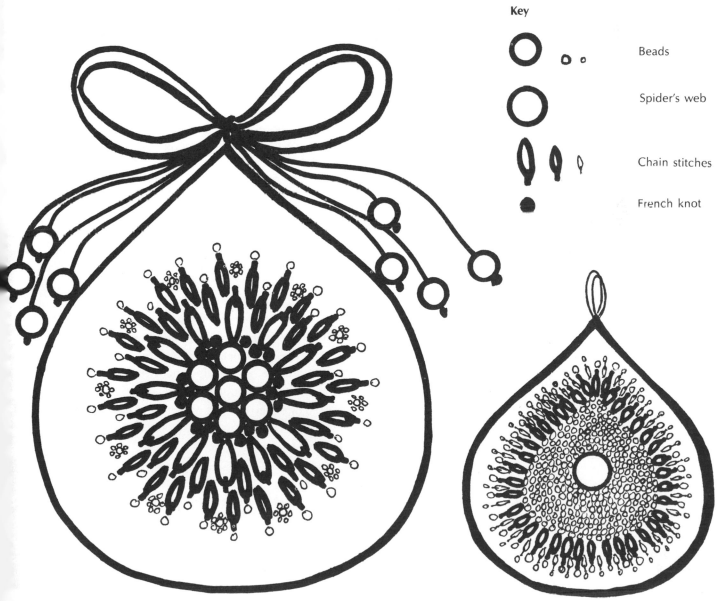

Beads

Spider's web

Chain stitches

French knot

63

6. Work a row of single chain stitches in 2 strands of stranded cotton around the row of loops, putting a bead at the end of each stitch.

To make up:

1. Cut the card or plastic to the shape of the pendant.

2. Fold the embroidered fabric over this and glue to the back.

3. Glue a small loop of ribbon to the top of the pendant and a tassel of beads and ribbons to the lower centre.

4. Cut a piece of suede, felt or thin leather a fraction smaller than the pendant and glue to the back.

The Bag

You will need:

1. A piece of velvet 30 cm × 15 cm.
2. Lining the same size.
3. Thin wadding 30 cm × 30 cm.
4. 1 metre each of 2 colours of 3 mm silk or polyester ribbon.
5. 1 metre of 3 mm satin ribbon.
6. 2 metres of 1.5 mm satin ribbon.
7. Beads in the same colours as the pendant.
8. Stranded cotton to match the velvet.
9. 15 large beads in a contrast colour.

Method:

1. Cut the piece of velvet into two pieces 15 cm × 15 cm.

2. In the centre of one piece sew 7 large beads in a circle with one in the centre.

3. Work single chains around this in satin ribbon.

4. Work French knots in 6 strands of stranded cotton between these stitches and the beads.

5. Work two more rows of single chains in silk ribbon, working them between the previous row.

6. Sew a bead with a circle of beads around it at the end of the satin ribbon chains.

7. Sew a bead at the end of each other chain.

To make up:

1. Cut 4 pieces of thin wadding the exact shape of the bag.

2. Cut the embroidered velvet and lining 1.5 cm larger.

3. Fold each piece of velvet and each piece of lining over a cut shape of wadding and stitch by hand, taking care not to take the stitches through to the front.

4. Sew the lining to each half of the outside of the bag, sewing it first inside the outside edge with a slip stitch.

5. Sew the two halves of the bag together with ladder stitch. Leave an opening at the top large enough to take the pendant easily.

6. Sew two lengths of fine ribbon to each side of the top of the bag, sewing the ribbons in the centre. Thread beads onto the ribbons and knot.

Chrysanthemum Brooch and Bag

The chrysanthemums are worked in silk ribbons on moire taffeta with gold beads making rich centres to the flowers.

The bag can be used as a container for the brooch or for other jewellery such as chains or pearls. It can also be used as a cosmetic purse.

You will need:

1. A piece of fabric 42 cm × 24 cm.
2. A piece of thin wadding 36 cm × 12 cm.
3. 4 metres each of 2 close shades of silk ribbon 3 mm wide.
4. Perle cotton number 8 for stems and leaves.
5. Gold beads.
6. Sewing thread to match the fabric.
7. Oval brooch mount (obtainable at craft shops).
8. Fabric glue.

Method:

1. Cut 6 cm off the length of the fabric. This will be for the brooch.

2. Press the fabric in half lengthwise, making a piece 12 cm × 36 cm.

3. Open out and at the centre of the right hand side of one end and about 9 cm in, mark in pencil dots an oval the size of the large chrysanthemum, with another small oval for the centre of the flower. Mark dotted lines for the stems.

4. Work curled petals (see diagram on page 22) in the two shades of silk ribbon, working a section at a time. Make straight stitches in twisted ribbon at the back of the flower.

5. Fill the centre with beads, and sew some around the flower.

6. Work the profile flower and bud in short curls, adding beads outside.

7. With Perle cotton number 8 work the stems and leaves in stem stitch.

To make up:

1. Place a piece of wadding 34 cm × 9 cm on the wrong side of one half of the fabric.

2. Turn the fabric over the wadding and press.

3. Fold the other half of the fabric onto the padded side, turn under the seam allowances to match and press.

4. Ladder stitch around the edges.

5. Fold one-third of the length up and oversew the sides with neat small stitches with matching thread.

For the Brooch:

1. Cut an oval of thin card slightly smaller than the size of the brooch.

2. Work a chrysanthemum on the fabric, in a size that will fill the shape of the brooch.

3. Cut the embroidered fabric 1 cm larger than the card.

4. Run a running stitch around the edge, centre the embroidery over the card, pull up firmly and fasten off securely.

5. Fit the embroidery into the brooch mount to see that it fits well. Make any adjustments.

6. Glue the embroidery into the mount with fabric glue.

Key

Chrysanthemum petal

 Beads

 Stem stitch

Waratah Brooch and Bag

The waratah, a spectacular Australian native plant, is the emblem for New South Wales.

This brooch and its matching bag would make a charming gift for an overseas visitor or friend. It has been worked on velveteen with silk and satin ribbons and beads, both round and square ended.

Designs of other native flowers could be worked in a similar way.

To make the set illustrated you will need:

1. A piece of velveteen 10 cm × 20 cm.
2. A piece of fabric for lining 10 cm × 16 cm.
3. 1 piece of thin wadding 10 cm × 16 cm.
4. 2 m each of two shades of 3 mm red silk ribbon.
5. 1 m (1 yard) each of two shades of 3 mm satin ribbon.
6. Red beads, both round and square ended, have been used in the illustrated set, but round beads only would be quite satisfactory.
7. Green stranded cotton.
8. Sewing cotton to match the velveteen and red satin ribbons.
9. A brooch mount.
10. A small piece of card the size of the brooch mount.
11. Fabric glue.

Method:

Cut two pieces 10 cm × 8 cm from the velveteen.

2. On one of these pieces mark the outline of the 3 waratahs with a water soluble fabric marking pen, making a dotted line.

3. With the red silk ribbons work a few straight stitches to define the lower half of the waratahs, making this section a little over half of the shape. Use more of the darker shade of ribbon.

4. Make some twisted curls with the silk ribbons, over the straight stitches (see instructions for the chrysanthemum on page 22).

5. Bead the top half of the flowers, working the outline first and then sewing the beads between the previous row, brick fashion.

6. Add 2 or 3 curls in silk ribbon, bringing them over the beaded section.

7. Make 4 or 5 straight stitches from the outside into the lower centre of the flower, using the red satin ribbons. Leave these stitches fairly loose, and twist them a little. Sew them in place with matching sewing cotton.

8. Work leaves in fly stitch with one strand of stranded cotton.

9. Work one waratah and leaves on the remaining velveteen for the brooch.

To make up the brooch:

1. Cut the card so that it will fit loosely into the brooch mount.

65

Key

● ● ●   Beads

                 Curls

                 Twisted straight stitches

                 Two rows of fly stitches

2. Cut the embroidered fabric for the brooch about 1 cm larger than the card and run a running stitch around the edge.

3. Centre the embroidery over the card, draw up the running stitch until the fabric fits firmly over the card. Fasten off securely.

4. Check to see that the covered card fits snugly in the mount, and make any adjustments.

5. Apply some glue to the back of the covered card, spread with a darning needle. Fit the embroidery into the mount and press firmly.

To make up the bag:

1. Cut two oval shapes in the thin wadding, exactly the size of the bag. Cut the two pieces of velveteen, one embroidered, 1 cm larger.

2. Cut two oval pieces of lining fabric the same size.

3. Cover the wadding shapes with the velveteen. Gather around the curves to achieve a smooth finish.

4. Press lightly into a well padded surface.

5. Turn in the edge of the lining pieces and sew neatly to the prepared velveteen sides.

6. Sew the two sides of the bag together with ladder stitch, leaving an opening large enough to take the brooch.

7. Attach 20 cm of the red satin ribbon to each side of the bag at the centre of the opening, use both shades of ribbon, one on each side.

Note: The bag illustrated fastens with a bow at the lower centre. This is deliberate, as the bow finishes the design and would look odd at the top.

Wattle Brooch and Bag

A design from another Australian shrub makes this delightful brooch and bag set.

The design is illustrated on a polyester and cotton fabric in silk ribbon, beads and stranded cotton and the bag is lined with silk.

For the set, you will need:

1. A piece of fabric 22 cm × 10 cm.
2. A piece of lining fabric 20 cm × 10 cm.
3. A piece of thin wadding 20 cm × 10 cm.
4. 1 metre of 3 mm green silk or soft polyester ribbon.
5. Yellow beads.
6. Green and yellow stranded cotton.
7. 0.5 metre green satin ribbon 1.5 mm wide.
8. A brooch mount.
9. Card the size of the mount.
10. Fabric glue.
11. Sewing cotton to match the fabric.

Method:

1. From the fabric cut two shapes for the bag allowing 1 cm turnings.
2. On both pieces mark a series of dots, in pencil or water soluble fabric marking pen, following the central line of the design as illustrated.
3. Work the wattle flowers in beads, adding French knots at the ends of the sprays in three strands of stranded cotton.
4. Work straight stitches in the green silk ribbon.
5. Work fly stitches in one strand of stranded cotton around the straight stitches.
6. Work the design on the remaining fabric for the brooch.

To make up:

For the brooch, follow the same instructions as for the waratah brooch.

For the bag:

1. Follow the instructions for the waratah bag. Sew the two halves of the bag together, leaving a section at the top to form the flap.
2. Sew a small loop of satin ribbon to the centre of the flap and a 22 cm length of the same ribbon to the front to correspond to the loop. Thread one end of this ribbon through the loop and tie a bow.

Key

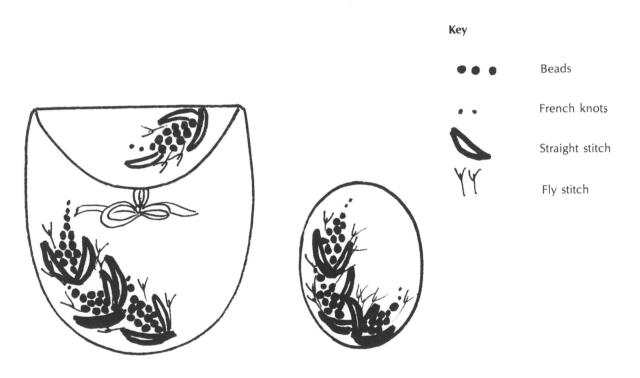

● ● ●	Beads
● ●	French knots
	Straight stitch
Y Y	Fly stitch

Small Gifts

Tissue Holder

The tissue holder is for purse-size packets of tissues. It is best made in a firm fabric, which should be washable.

The design is simple to work as it consists of chain stitch and French knots only.

You will need:

1. A piece of fabric 30 cm × 14 cm.
2. 1 metre each of 3 mm satin ribbon and two shades of silk or soft polyester ribbon.
3. Shiny thread or stranded cotton to tone with the ribbons.
4. Stranded cotton in a contrast colour.
5. Sewing cotton to match the fabric.

Method:

1. Fold the piece of fabric in half, then fold again so that the first fold lies on the stitching line at the raw edge. Press the fold firmly. If the fabric is springy, baste a line on the fold. The embroidery is worked between the centre fold and the two outer folds and should be approximately 1.5 cm from the outer fold.

2. Work the two lines of embroidery, starting with the satin ribbon, then the silk ribbons, followed by chain stitch in a shiny thread, and the French knots. The leaf design is in opposite directions each side of the opening of the tissue holder.

3. Seam the two raw edges, right sides together. Press seam open.

4. Turn to the right side and fold in and press the side edges. The seam should lie in the centre on the reverse side to the embroidery.

5. With the embroidery to the inside, fold the edges to the centre. They should just meet.

6. Stitch across the ends.

7. Turn to the right side and press carefully, with the embroidery face down.

8. Stitch each side of the opening together with a few neat stitches, and insert tissues.

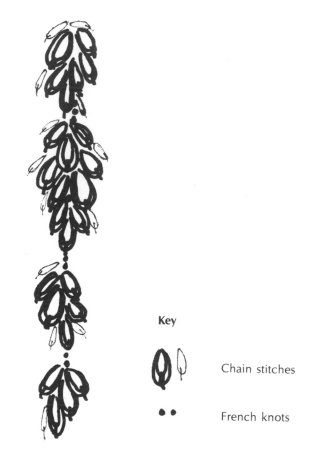

Key

Chain stitches

French knots

Tissue holder

68

Spectacle Cleaner

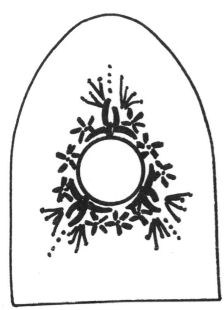

Cut 2 in plastic or card

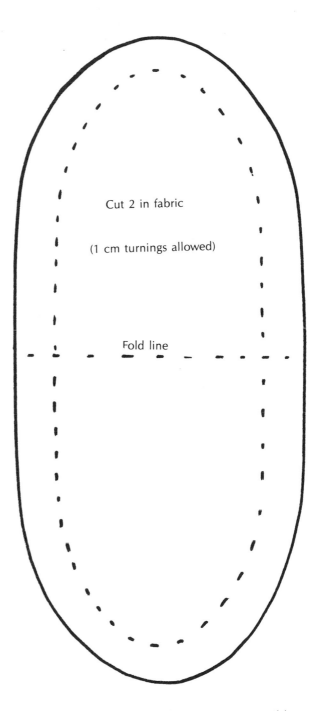

Cut 2 in fabric

(1 cm turnings allowed)

Fold line

Key

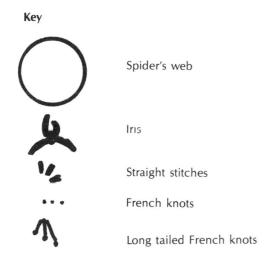

Spider's web

Iris

Straight stitches

French knots

Long tailed French knots

You will need:

1. Piece of fabric 18 cm X 15 cm approx.
2. Piece of chamois leather 16 cm X 7 cm approx.
3. Piece of plastic from ice cream carton 15 cm X 12 cm approx.
4. 0.5 metre of 5 mm satin ribbon.
5. 1 metre each of 2 colours in 3 mm silk or soft polyester ribbon.
6. Stranded cotton in 3 shades.
7. 0.5 metre of 1 cm satin or nylon ribbon.
8. 1 large bead with a large hole.

Method:

1. Cut out plastic, fabric and chamois leather according to the pattern.
2. Work embroidery on one half of one piece of fabric, starting with the spider's web in 5 mm satin ribbon, then irises in silk or polyester ribbon. The small flowers are next, also in silk ribbon with French knots in the centre. The French knots and long tailed French knots are worked last, in 3 strands of stranded cotton.

3. Place one piece of plastic in the centre of the reverse side of the embroidered fabric. Run a gathering thread around the curved part of the shape, and pull up till the fabric fits over the plastic.

4. Lace across the back from side to side until the fabric is taut around the plastic.

5. Fold remaining half of the fabric over the reverse side, turn under and hem neatly just inside the edge of the shape.

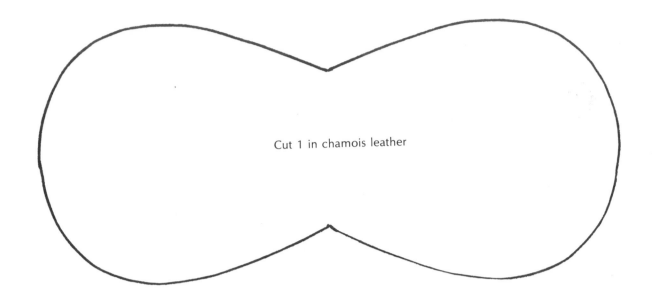

Cut 1 in chamois leather

Spectacle cleaner

6. Repeat 3 to 5 with the other piece of fabric.

7. Sew two halves together, starting 0.5 cm from centre top and using a slanting stitch in 3 strands of stranded cotton to match the fabric. On reaching the lower edge stitch back over the stitches to form a cross stitch. Repeat on the other side.

8. Thread the 1 cm ribbon through the centre of the chamois leather and, using a long darning needle, through the hole in the top of the case.

9. Thread both ends of ribbon through a bead and tie a knot behind it.

Note: The ribbon should extend about 8 cm, plus bead, from the top of the case when the chamois leather is pulled inside it.

This makes a very attractive and useful gift for anyone who wears glasses. It is small enough to be carried in purse or pocket.

Chatelaine

A chatelaine, worn around the neck while sewing, is a very special gift for someone who enjoys needlework. The two large hearts form needlecase and pincushion; the small one holds a thimble.

You will need:

1. Card or fabric from an ice cream container.
2. Fabric (silk is nice for a special gift).
3. 2 metres of 3 mm satin ribbon in 2 shades.
4. 2 metres of 3 mm soft ribbon in a toning shade.
5. Perle cotton numbers 5 and 8.
6. Stranded cotton in a contrast colour.
7. Small amount of thin wadding.
8. Small scrap of flannel.

9. 1.5 metres of 10 mm floral ribbon to tone with the embroidery.
10. 1.5 metres of 10 mm plain ribbon to tone with the floral ribbon.
11. Sewing cotton to match the fabric.
12. Fabric glue.
13. Selection of needles.
14. Pearl or glass headed pins.
15. Thimble.
16. Embroidery scissors.

Method:

1. Cut out 6 large hearts in fabric, as in the diagram, allowing 1 cm turning all round.

2. Embroider the design in two hearts, taking care to centre the design. Attach heart shaped pieces of flannel, slightly smaller than the large heart, to two other hearts.

3. Cut 4 smaller fabric hearts, as in the diagram, allowing 1 cm turnings.

4. Embroider one.

5. Cut 6 large hearts and 4 smaller ones from card or plastic and 7 large and 2 small from thin wadding.

6. Lightly glue the wadding to the plastic or card hearts.

7. Cover the wadding with the fabric, carefully making small cuts in the curves so that the edges fold over the edges of the card or plastic.

8. Glue the fabric to the back only. Use the minimum amount of a good fabric glue and apply it to the back of the card or plastic with a large darning needle.

You should now have 6 large hearts, 2 embroidered, 2 with flannel, and 2 plain, and 4 small hearts, one embroidered and the others plain. There should be a heart in wadding over.

9. Machine stitch the floral and plain ribbon together. This makes an attractive and strong ribbon on which to attach the hearts.

10. Glue one plain large heart 15 cm from one end of the floral ribbon, and one 30 cm from the other end.

11. Glue one small plain heart over the 15 cm end.

12. Next, place the spare wadding heart, trimmed slightly, on one of the plain hearts. Cover it with an embroidered heart and ladder stitch together. This is the pincushion and should have pins stuck round it.

13. Glue short lengths of 10 mm ribbon to the points of the other plain large heart and embroidered large heart. This forms a hinge for the needle case.

14. Glue a loop of 3 mm satin ribbon to the centre top of the embroidered heart.

15. Then ladder stitch the two hearts with flannel to these two hearts.

16. Cover a button with a circle of fabric and work a spider's web rose on it; sew the button to the floral ribbon just above the needle case, so that the needlecase can be closed by the ribbon loop over the button.

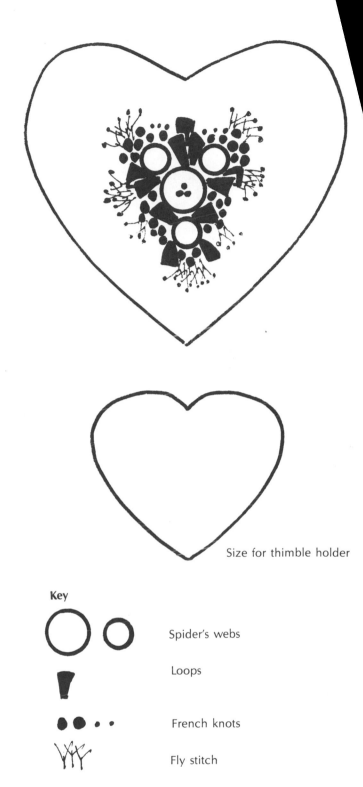

Size for thimble holder

Key

⭕ ⭕   Spider's webs

▼   Loops

●● ··   French knots

ᙁᙁ   Fly stitch

17. Next, glue a small length of ribbon to the small embroidered heart. It should be long enough to fit over the thimble which is held in by it.

18. Sew the other two plain hearts to these with ladder stitch, then ladder stitch the two lined halves together. Sew a press fastener to the ribbon tab and to the ribbon above the heart.

71

Chatelaine—needleholder, pincushion, thimble holder and scissors

19. Pass the 30 cm end of floral ribbon through the handles of a pair of embroidery scissors and sew the end 11.5 cm up the ribbon. The scissors should be able to be opened easily.

20. Add a selection of needles to the flannel in the needle case and the chatelaine is finished.